To Elinor,

Best wishes,

Evelyn Dalby

2019

It's Not Easy Being A Pelican

Written by Evelyn Dabritz
Illustrated by Isobel Hoffman

CENTRAL COAST PRESS
P.O. BOX 3654
SAN LUIS OBISPO, CALIFORNIA 93403

Evelyn & David Dabritz
3650 Studio Dr.
Cayucos, CA 93430-1943
seasidestories@gmail.com

Other books by Evelyn Dabritz:
"Bonnie Barnacle Finds a Home" - 2007;
"How the Innkeeper Worm Got a Full House" - 2009;
"Kelp Condo Crisis" - 2010

The printing of this book was funded
in part by a grant from the
Morro Bay
National Estuary Program
which is a program of the
U. S. Environmental Protection Agency.

Ink drawing courtesy Genie Over

Dear Readers:

This story is about the life cycle of the brown pelican. It is a mixture of facts and fantasy ("faction") with accurate information. It is my hope that the story will not only teach, but will create an interest and appreciation for the wonders of nature. Those of you reading to younger children have the opportunity to interpret and to further their vocabulary development as well.

Evelyn Dabritz

This book is especially dedicated to my husband, David Dabritz, who believed in my stories and urged me on. Also, this book is dedicated, with love, to my children, Robert, John, Karl, and Dorothy, and to my grandchildren, Jessica, Kyle, and Tyler, who listened to Grandma's stories. Included in this dedication are the teachers who love to teach about nature and the parents who read to their children.

The California Brown Pelican
Pelecanus occidentalis californicus

It is always a thrill to look up and see a V-formation flight of pelicans. They skillfully master the air currents almost effortlessly.

Fossils show that pelicans have been around for millions of years with very little change. Pelicans have some unique characteristics that differ from other bird families. The pouch hanging from the long beak can expand to hold up to 3 gallons of water as the bird nets fish. Pelicans cannot straighten their necks because the 7th, 8th, and 9th vertebrae are fused. The birds have four webbed toes instead of the usual three of the other web-footed birds.

There are seven species of pelicans in the pelican family *Pelecanidae.*

The California Brown Pelican is smaller than other pelican species, weighing 8-11 pounds and with a wingspan of 7 feet. Brown Pelicans are the only pelicans that plunge dive from heights up to 100 feet into the water to net fish. Special air sacs help to absorb the impact of hitting the water. Brown Pelicans make the most elaborate plumage changes of any bird in their yearly cycle of breeding, nesting, and molting.

California Brown Pelicans nest mostly on islands off the coast of California in the spring. They move over the coastal waters and estuaries from Baja to British Columbia following the schools of mainly anchovies and sardines and mackerel.

In the 1960's the sharp decline of pelicans led to the discovery that the pesticide, DDT, was responsible for the thinning of their egg shells. They were put on the endangered species list in the 1970's and have made a strong comeback with the banning of DDT.

During the first year it is not easy being a pelican. Many die from broken necks while learning to dive; and some from lack of fishing skills during this perilous time.

Mr. Pelican circled the island just off the coast of California. With his great wings which spread over six feet, he skillfully rode the air currents, gliding and using a powerful stroke only now and then. Winter is the time of the year when brown pelicans return to the colony. Hundreds of other brown pelicans were already there claiming nests. He saw an area where several nests had not been taken.

Touching down gracefully, he folded his wings and waddled clumsily. There were hollowed mounds of dirt, sea weed, grasses, and twigs left over from previous years. Here was one several inches high that would need only a few repairs. He knew Mrs. Pelican would be happy when she saw it.

When Mrs. Pelican flew in, she was attracted by Mr. Pelican's wonderful display. She sat for a while admiring the way he moved his head back and forth sideways in a figure eight. Finally, she waddled over to greet him. Their meeting was very serious and quiet since adult pelicans make very few sounds. Their joy was shown with head and body movements.

What a handsome couple they made, feathered in their brightest colors for this courtship time. Their heads were bright yellow. The skin around their yellow eyes was bright pink. Their enormous beaks were shades of orange with a black pouch hanging below. White necks, grayish-brown backs and wings, and black bellies completed their colorful dress. They were beautiful to each other, even if they might seem a bit comical. It was a time for just enjoying each other's company.

Enough of that, it was early spring and time to work on the nest. Mr. Pelican flew off and soon returned with a twig that he presented to Mrs. Pelican as a loving gift. She accepted the twig as if it were a bouquet of flowers and worked it into just the right place. Mr. Pelican returned again and again with twigs, grasses, and even sea weed.

Mrs. Pelican worked hard shaping the nest and making it cozy. They made sure that neighboring nests were no closer than an outstretched bill. With other couples so close, it was important to guard the nest from pelicans too lazy to get their own nesting materials. They snapped their bills and flapped their wings when it was necessary to discourage "nestnappers".

What a happy day it was when Mrs. Pelican laid her first chalky white egg. Two days later a second egg arrived, and then a third. It was fulltime duty for the proud parents. They took turns sitting on the nest. They even used their large webbed feet to keep the eggs warm. The eggs had to be shaded from the hot sun and protected from the gulls that robbed nests. One day Mrs. Pelican stood up to stretch a bit. Before she knew what was happening, a greedy gull swooped down, rolled an egg out of the nest, and cracked it open.

One could tell that it was almost time for the eggs to hatch by looking at the changing colors of the parents. Their bright yellow heads were turning white and their necks were turning a dark, chocolate brown. Even their yellow eyes turned brown. These complicated color changes continuing through the year make pelicans fashion leaders in the bird world. After chicks leave the nest, adult colors change again, and molting replaces old, shabby feathers.

After nearly a month of incubating, the first egg cracked and out flopped an ugly, naked, blind, helpless girl chick.

Mr. Pelican looked anxiously at the new arrival. "Oh, my dear, do you think she's all right?"

"Don't worry, dear, she'll be stronger when she gets lots of food. Just give her a couple of weeks and that ugly, gray, wrinkled skin will be covered with a soft, white down," assured Mrs. Pelican.

"What shall we name her?" asked Mr. Pelican.

"Patty Pelican has a good ring. You had better go fishing for her first meal!" said Mrs. Pelican excitedly.

Mr. Pelican took off and soon returned. "What do I do now, Mrs. Pelican?"

"Just bring up some of your partially digested fish and dribble it down your bill in front of her," instructed Mrs. Pelican.

Mr. Pelican finally got his big bill in position and patiently dribbled food so that Patty could scoop it up. It was all Patty could do to scoop up her meal. She fell back into a sound sleep.

"This isn't easy!" said Mr. Pelican, somewhat flustered.

"Just be patient. Soon her eyes will be open, and she'll be able to grab food out of your beak," encouraged Mrs. Pelican.

In two more days the second egg hatched and a little boy chick flopped out, equally ugly and helpless.

It was Mr. Pelican's turn to think of a name. "Let's call him Paul. Yes, Paul Pelican sounds just right."

By now, the usually quiet nesting colony was alive with the loud screaming, grunting, and clucking of hundreds of chicks begging for food. The sky was filled with pelican parents gliding in and taking off. Noisy gulls darted in and out, trying to grab eggs and chicks. Patty and Paul added their shrill cries for food. Now, when a parent brought in food, they pushed and flapped their wings trying to be the first to be fed. It looked as if they were being swallowed as they grabbed fish tidbits out of those big bills. Paul was smaller than Patty, but he was soon able to hold his own in the scramble for food.

The noise was bad enough for the hardworking parents, but sometimes neighboring chicks waddled into their nest begging and shrieking.

"Why can't our neighbors keep those begging babies at home?" complained Mr. Pelican. "This noise is enough to give us headaches."

In ten weeks Patty and Paul were bigger than their parents. They still had white bellies, but their backs, heads, and necks had turned brown. Feathers had replaced the down.

The weary parents had a hard time supplying two to three pounds of fish a day for each chick. To satisfy their own appetites, each parent also needed about four pounds of fish a day. Sometimes they had to fly twenty to thirty miles to find good schools of fish.

"It won't be long until you'll be catching your own fish," said Mr. Pelican hopefully.

"Be sure to exercise your wings," advised Mrs. Pelican. "You are beginning to look grubby. You'll never be able to fly if you don't take better care of your feathers. Use the hook on your bill to preen your feathers. For the feathers you can't reach, use that special hook you have on your third toe."

Patty was ready for her first flight. She flapped her wings, pushed off with her feet, and rose above the colony. "Whee, this is fun!" she thought. "Oh, look at the view! It's so peaceful away from all of that noise and no little brother to pester me."

She circled and realized that she would have to land sometime. Down, down she glided as the nesting area rose to meet her. "This is not easy," she thought as her feet wobbled back and forth. Bam! She crashed into a ledge on the cliff. Several gulls shrieked with laughter as she picked herself up and straightened her ruffled feathers.

Paul had been watching his sister's first attempt. This made him even more nervous about flying, but he was determined. "Well, here goes!" he said bravely. Soon he, too, was experiencing the thrill of soaring and gliding above the colony. His landing was even fairly smooth.

"Patty, let's join that group flying over to the next island. We sure need the practice," called Paul. "Look, they are flying in a V-formation."

They took positions near the back of the V, trying hard to keep the correct distance and time their wingbeats. It wasn't easy, but the leader was very patient. Next, it was time for Follow the Leader. They flew down single file as their line curved and dipped just over the waves.

"Just feel the lift of the wave. We hardly have to flap," called Paul happily.

Suddenly, the wave broke, catching Paul and slamming him into the surf. After tumbling around a bit, he popped right up and paddled along. Before the next wave caught him, he managed to struggle back into the air.

Paul and Patty were tired, but very excited about their experiences. Suddenly, Paul said, "I'm getting hungry! Where are Mom and Dad?"

"Don't you remember? They said it was time for us to catch our own fish," Patty called.

"You mean they're not going to help us anymore? That diving looks awfully hard to do," said Paul nervously.

"Silly, just watch me. It can't be that hard. We've been watching pelicans dive for days," Patty yelled as she climbed upward where she could look for a school of fish.

Patty was gliding along about twenty feet above the water when she spotted several fish just under the surface of the water. "If only I can remember how other pelicans do this," she thought, trying to picture the correct moves. She slowed, then plunged down with her wings spread out. At the last moment before she hit the water, she folded her wings back halfway, stretched out her neck, and shot her feet back. Splat! She hit the water with a big splash. "Oh, that hurt!" she cried, holding her neck a little to the side. Not even her special air sacs had cushioned her head enough that time. There was no fish, either.

Paul said, "I don't think I can do that."

"Well, you had better try," said Patty. "Mother said we might have to go live with the white pelicans if we don't learn to dive. They don't even know how to dive. They just swim around and scoop up the fish."

"Well, I don't want to do that. It's not easy being a brown pelican, but I'll hang in there and try," said Paul bravely.

When Paul managed to overcome his fear, he flew above the water and spotted some fish. It was a perfect dive! He opened his bill, netted a fish, and turned completely over under the water. "I got one! I got one!" he thought excitedly. He righted himself, pointed his bill down, and was draining nearly two gallons of water from his elastic pouch. Just as he was opening his bill to turn the fish around, a gull swooped down and grabbed his fish.

"Thanks for the fish!" taunted the thieving gull as it sped away.

Poor Paul could only watch as his fish disappeared down the gull's throat.

"Oh, I'm really hungry now," said Patty. "I don't see any more fish, and I'm too tired to try diving again."

"Oh, look down there, Patty! There's a boat throwing out fish scraps. Let's fly over there!" called Paul.

The two hungry chicks flew down near the boat and scooped up fish scraps as the fishermen cleaned fish. It wasn't long until both chicks were full.

"I wish we could take back some of these scraps in our bills," said Patty, "but I know we can't take off with full pouches. Mother always told us not to fly with our mouths full."

"That was lucky! We'll have to try fishing again tomorrow. There won't always be a fishing boat to follow. We won't give up," said Paul.

They worked at diving the next day and finally managed to catch one fish each. As time went on they were able to catch fish more often in their dives. They found that they could fly near the surface of the water and occasionally scoop up a fish with a shallow dive. Patty and Paul lost weight, but their fishing skills were improving daily. At last they were rewarded with a fish on almost every dive.

It was now time for the pelicans to migrate to the Coast. Patty and Paul decided to join a group of young pelicans that were flying off to the Central Coast waters and estuaries. They flew away from their little island on a new adventure. It isn't easy being a pelican, but they had passed the test for survival.

As they approached the mainland shore, they spotted a large school of fish. What a pelican party began as pelicans plunged again and again into the water for fish.

Patty and Paul would never be lonely. There would always be flocks of pelican friends for flying, fishing, nesting, or loafing. Winter would bring them back to the island colony. In about three years they would be raising their own families.

Evelyn Dabritz (right) is a retired teacher. She is a docent for the Morro Bay Museum of Natural History. Her love of natural science is shared with hundreds of boys and girls who visit the museum on school field trips.

Roaming in the woods as a child at her home in northwestern Washington instilled a love of nature.

Isobel Hoffman (left) enjoyed a much-traveled childhood, during which her family visited parks, museums, and zoos of many cities, states, and several countries. This instilled a lifelong fascination with the biology of our beautiful world.

Retired from parenting and textbook editing, she became a docent at The Morro Bay Museum of Natural History.